750

INSTANT KILLER WIG
Dan Kaplan

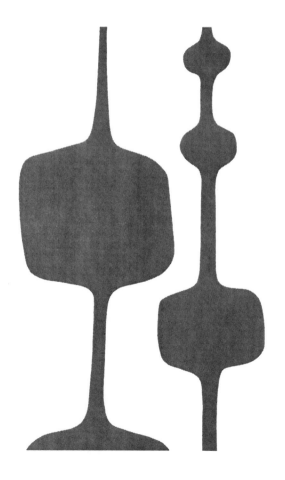

SPUYTEN DUYVIL

NEW YORK CITY

ISBN 978-1-944682-96-5

Cover Art: Susie Steele

Library of Congress Cataloging-in-Publication Data

Names: Kaplan, Dan, 1971- author.
Title: Instant killer wig / Dan Kaplan.
Description: New York City : Spuyten Duyvil, [2018]
Identifiers: LCCN 2017038942 | ISBN 9781944682965
Classification: LCC PS3611.A648 A6 2018 | DDC 811/.6--dc23
LC record available at https://lccn.loc.gov/2017038942

The fact that I cannot imagine the present moment has always worried me.

—Miroslav Holub

+

I have been in a good mood recently but not really.

Which is precisely it.

Every year the trees are heavier, like they know something
and haven't been away.

For most of us it is the same time every day, when we draw
the shades.

Arriving there with bouquets in each hand for we can't
remember what.

The bulk of interference comes from chemistry and the
elements and what follows us around in combination.

The sky was dreaming cloud cover and we were the ones
staging it. As if put upon.

Never accounting for what is seasonally adjusted.

For the thirty thousandth time, a person said, go feed
yourself. And was close.

The trouble with patterns is how they appear years later.

Floral and chainlink coming to mind.

When the background pushes forward and we with our feet
halt the throw rugs and reach for the tumblers.

In our spaces, what lives undetected.

The left lung a touch smaller than the right, for example.
To make room for the heart.

It sounds worse than it is, it is true.

You can and always have heard the highway from here—
just realized.

Which changes things.

If one can picture cargo en route.

And the slopes in some distance.

Though I wouldn't go that far.

+

There is a glass of water
in each loaf of bread.

If we took away all of the water
a watermelon would only be as big
as a few bones.

If we were to set a fire
under a box full of bees
the bees would fly out of the box
and into the air.

If things are heated
they spread out and get
just a little bigger.

There are whole days.

Landing on some dry leaves,
they begin to burn.

You can make ashtrays
or animals or dolls.

Your bathing suit will dry very quickly.

If two dogs begin running
in circles, there will be two boys
in the center.

If falling, can you believe
the snow.

+

My favorite character in the United Airlines safety video
is the narrator. In particular, his beard is something

to speak of. It's almost as though he doesn't have a beard,
the way he positions his face. And yet he does.

The boy whose mother secures her oxygen mask first—
we can't overlook him either. His patience in the face

of danger we could all learn from. Every time I see that,
the mother attending to herself before her child—well,

it feels wrong. It's good, for that reason, neither
has a speaking part. Only the bearded man does.

The business traveler, who is animated, doesn't even have
a mouth. Some, like the floatation-device demonstrator

and her seatmate, appear to be chatting—about what
we can't hear. The sound might not have been recorded

or it was but cut later. Or it could be they were mouthing
words, pretending to hold conversation before the emergency.

+

What you are made of is
immaterial.

Without a doubt, if you had one,
a plate would be grand.

Rehearsal, for the life of me,
is when I perform best.

As expected, the advice is lie back
to the sun.

Why is Cher almost always
the answer!

Swimming this afternoon,
my nerves are showing.

In the heat, everything reaches
for the breeze.

You are on a horse thinking
about this.

If you make a suggestion, I will take
your word for it. Promise.

+

An average day takes at least 3 of us.

To erect the poles and scenery.

The equipment checks and parties on all sides
accounted for.

Breaking for lunch while another hemisphere is torn down.

Our pails rattling with vegetables and staples
which hold us together.

On location at the site of future accidents and children
with both hands stopping us to demonstrate.

With night falling and the conversations turning elsewhere
to sleep.

In the language of time zones, bedding down

before we are ready.

+

For a time known as "the little gem of the citrus family"
the *kumquat* (or *cumquat*, or *comquot*, or *kunquat*, or *kin*,
or *kin kan*, or *kin kit*, or *kin kuit*, or *kuit xu*, or *chu tsu*,
or *chantu*) was in 1915 placed in the genus *fortunella*
by the agricultural botanist Walter T. Swingle.

+

What has gotten into you.

Afternoons like this, they are big in our eyes
and tend to live on the skin.

If light makes it through then
I hope you can sleep.

Who is attending to this place.

Think of the right person
and what he could do.

You have been holding up your end for an eternity.
Would you like a hand.

Now I am regretting my passing
and not getting off at the last stop.

Perhaps you would prefer storing by your feet
over your head.

Yes, it is fitting. Thank you.

No, no. Think of nothing.

+

Photography became a close collaborator. As the picture at left suggests,

identical bears raid minivans at Yellowstone. Two small girls appear
in stereo photographs, 1853. One drops her nightgown on the way

to the tub, the other falls from a window. At one time

such enlargements are difficult, costly. At one time
trucks cart quarter-ton glass plates over bumps through the desert

to catch a passing locomotive. When there are sandwiches for the crew

lazing in the brush, they are eaten. When the heavens pitch

Orion brushes the eye. The white circle at the center
signifies what the eye will tolerate as suitably focused.

+

Think of a plumber between 1 and 10. Would you prefer to lay down.

I applaud the wallpaper. I could plant myself here and watch the hours glow.

Water would be fine.

It seems these days one cannot keep a foot in. Is that window already closed. In all likelihood a cannonball will follow.

People can't recall it worries me. Is it a given. Is that an expression.

Look, the moon is finished.

You would like a pimento. Place it in the martini, butterfingers, but first wipe the surface.

I am ill suited. It is clear.

Do not be strained. What you possess was boxed and shipped from reception.

Such heights. The questions I have include why children are here.

Such cheek. What use if you cannot find time. I have had it.

+

The experiment in which everything was different
by an inch went pretty much as expected:

the missed handshakes, the tripping,
the paint buckets and catapulting David Hasselhoff

mugs, the door frames knocking us back.
The shin and noggin rubbing: vigorous.

In short, there were bandages.
Though we'd never use these particular words,

object and *proximity* became the topic,
summarized by the paper cuts and tongue

lashings we received, the commuters with half
mustaches, the clouds gone sumo.

And yet on continents everywhere
a fragile peace was achieved

when the takeout boxes we launched actually landed
in the garbage. The trick: aim where you think

you'll miss. Direct the banana cream pie a tick left.
And yet winter after winter, straining the guard rails,

we live to tell. Naturally selected like the prehistoric
gecko in our atrium, we adjust, negotiate

the spaces, blissful in the preservation
of our side mirrors (objects closer than

they appear), groping our homes for the switches
we've flicked our lives over.

+

This requires something on our parts.

In light of the equipment
to which we are subject.

And that just such things
these days exist
in their heaviness.

Their clank and crumble
and shine.

Incumbency, from what we gather,
to make up this place.

The limbs and trunks
in our midst,

the cheese plate at the heart
of the buffet.

The canned good, the stock
some are prone to take.

+

While many stick on this point, a similar position
has been forwarded by the Beekeepers of America.
It behooves us to know where our honey comes from.

+

We are out of time and always
will be.

We pick our moment, take it slowly.

Once, the night a crushed carnation
at our feet.

Once, a sequined jacket at our backs.

The rest is secondary highway
and the trees lining it.

The information booth
and the clerk who needs a hug.

The cracked placard shining back facts.

Our questions regard us
from the rafters.

We want to be home
and at least the short-term good.

In drifts the underdressed season

reflecting both the seconds of history in which we reside
and the rest we need.

Around us, the rain shorts,
blinks on.

One among us braises. Another melts in
the clawfoot tub. And the fumbling

one with the rabbit ears,

the dials turning all static.

+

I never discuss love on an empty stomach.

It's one of those new apartments, wet paint and no telephone yet.

Each piece wrapped in gold paper.

It's not a very clear picture.

I'd invite you to my bedroom if I had a bedroom.

I always do when we're in session here.

My recommendation is still the same. We're not talking.

I mention it because the bed doesn't seem like it's been slept in.

It's something about my face. I have a big face.

It may not be cold enough.

I knew I should've served dinner earlier.

I never felt more alive.

I assumed Chicago.

I was wondering if I ought to change.

If you'd give this to one of the attendants in the public lounge.

If I might have a few words of parting.

I doubt if I'll see anybody else tonight.

The skin glow rehearsal's at noon.

+

Finished for the year with abdominal tear, groin strain, and hip flexor. Successful surgery to repair groin. Promising for upcoming season.

Season-ending injury to left thumb.

Surgery to repair torn adductor muscle. Full recovery next season expected.

Removed from action after collision which re-injured same ribs injured in a previous collision. Done for the season.

Sore foot. Surgery to insert screw to aid healing process. Remainder of season in doubt.

Two previous seasons missed with arm and leg injuries.

Surgery to repair tear of ulnar collateral ligament in right thumb. Lost for next season.

Surgery to remove bone chips in elbow.

Mild strain of upper pectoral muscle. Injury not serious but timetable uncertain.

Lower back stiffness. Tear in left and right hip. Future going forward in doubt.

+

Some polls suggest Tennessee is bigger than other states.
It's true.

My civic duty requires energy
half off.

Days lay down and grow
a flower.

Is it me or the crows
are exposing the trees.

Is that something or what
develops tonight!

At last the precipitation
we've been getting.

If you would alert me
we're here, please.

I think butterfly and pull
a muscle.

+

No animals were harmed
in the making of this
which is a relief
for the bleeding
heart in us
and good to boot
because we can't recollect
any in it to begin with.
The curb-jumping Corvette
flattening the hapless beagle,
the flummoxed chipmunk
negotiating the power grid:

they never happened.
Still, disclaimers are better
left for the finish.
Our breakfast, love
and tool-borrowing scenes
include nothing
gilled or furry
minus
a shower-curtain pattern
and some mascot tackling.
If they do,
tenderness rules.

+

Say your goodbyes.
We are here finally.

I was just commenting on
where time goes.

You are skin and bones
considering.

I do not feel
up to people today

and know what I would say
to seconds.

Would you stretch the date
until it snows.

Typically one sinks at midnight
then wipes the eyes and orbits.

Why is it blooming
on one side only.

Bless you.
I hear light.

+

We are not alone in this position.
A leg up, a finger on conditions.
Beside ourselves, we move our likenesses
from corner to corner to overhang,
the spiders in their complicated math
multiplying the factors—either
slip the errant limb or stomach
the wrecking ball. In the architecture
of gossamer we are taken lightly
from our posts and set out
on the breeze, the spiral and helix
mapping our drop. Cut or flooded
we wring and squeeze. We start
again. It's in our blood.

+

I can't say enough
about the olive and what
you have done with it

+

What is that jingle again.
Who is roofer to the world.

Re: Beethoven and the electric toothbrush:
not true.

Over the afternoon, masses
disagree with heat.

How easily it fits into
any briefcase or purse.

What we are asking for
is your wellbeing!

I will not tell you once.
Come home but don't upset the table.

I am always transported by flies
and a particular Buick.

And you.
Have you ever loomed.

I steam my broccoli as a matter
of fact.

+

While I have a relationship with my memories, I never date them.

Every now and then eating home for lunch, as do the most frugal.

Our flour-smeared appearance and decades tenderizing and seasoning.

The result being we in the blizzard very pink in Bermudas.

Such is the difficulty finding the weather under the circumstances.

Into our lots the needles dropping from evergreens.

The runners on every stairwell we are at pains to recover.

And overhead the glowing device. And everywhere the device

that otherwise opens and shuts.

+

Self esteem is trouble enough when exiting
the shower.

Nor in the light of hindsight should the reverse
beep be our soundtrack.

To the extent that later is vinyl retrospective and our 50+ features
pointed out.

Because when it comes to the movables, faces are far and away
the best at marking position.

Along the lines we draw and the better angles
of our nature.

The corners of the day turning back
but not like a negative.

Which is a reminder of certain passages and just what happens
when vegetables go bad.

Given what falls from the question as well as the question
of how long the season will last.

And just how different would it be without the flocking
or you, shotgun.

+

Someone has made off with my adage. Don me in something.

Perhaps you should comb the streets even. You spent your childhood here.

Where is the silver mine. How do you weigh it.

You are angry. Would you say opposite.

That is the maxim allowable. It depends on the procedure.

They swoop on occasions. Next season, as the last, will flood clots through this blue.

Tomorrow is a big day. If pressed, how would you stop.

That is a crack. Here is a daffodil. This is your best opportunity to make a right.

Are you better now that the door is latched. As children, what is your favorite activity.

I remember mostly, though the same I can say.

How moving. What is the feeling. Any advice at hand.

Draw on faces. Any scents.

Honey, do you have some. Some what.

+

I cannot accept flowers
but will open this morning.

Poised, everything is looking up.

Now I see those impressions
and where they come from.

I worry about reaching other bodies and feeling
like that moment's back.

So many formalities.

Many scientists believe humans
resent an interesting transition in time

and the explosion might leave a star.

O those above,
please don't cloud this peak.

+

Once we note how numbers change
appearances we try others.

The gray-headed albatross loops the globe
in 46 days and the extent of
migration is greater than thought.

Across the square
an ancient dog labors,
one day won't wake.

Night develops a faithful copy
others will scrape across.

As with certain advances
countries become little
more than geometries.

As small areas burn
and distant shapes occupy

something like fields
of vision.

+

Recently I have given thought to the United States
Postal Service and I am not sure how I feel. If it fits

it ships, claims the ad campaign. I think that's
what you call a series of advertisements or related

placements: a campaign. I like the sound of it as well as
the possibilities it presents. Much can be said

for both fitting and shipping. The real trouble
with mentioning it here is the tagline may have

changed by the time anyone sees this or it reaches
print. I am hopeful. But we do not all feel

this. Reaching print isn't what people say anymore.
I am not sure they ever did. Nowadays being current

seems more important than ever. Eventually
people come to feel this. Once I wrote about

a friend who is no longer a friend. It was never
my intention to mention him. Sometimes

one finds himself in situations. The letter carrier
in *Diva* gets caught in one. Cops and goons

pursue him for a tape he possesses. For a time
he eludes them. They want that tape.

+

What are the chances of a table tonight.

Something we could perhaps agree upon.

If memory serves
it is reserved.

Although now would happen
to be fine.

If not a damper in the past.

And just how sticky as the case may be
to put oneself out.

Things begin to grow on us.

There is a rash
and there is a stance.

And the progress to be sure.

So that by the time they arrive
the rains are behind us.

In fact it could be any number.

+

People, we are even younger than our picture.

Modeling behavior, some might have it,
for future generations.

One by one dropping into the days,
chipping the space.

The expression we are trying to place
is on a plane for Venice.

It goes without saying
children have smaller versions of them.

Given the constant reaching into the overhead
for whatever brings one comfort.

Statistics baring an aging population
and nothing less than full coverage
what we are looking for.

These days so commonly naked as
to be hardly remarkable.

The landscape pinned and wearing us
like an accessory.

And the lingering issue of how to address it
for the occasion.

Come dark, our sweeteners shift and settle,
our liquids shaped by their containers.

We hold ourselves together and attempt
this in various positions.

Close in the fields,
the clouds rising like a tent.

And outside and in
the animals particularly moving.

+

Rotating food is a suggestion.

+

What is the difference between an open coat and a closed coat?

Why are hole centers marked?

Would you list the principal uses of the arm?

What should be wrapped in newspaper?

What should you do before removing a guard from a machine?

Why is circling more accurate?

What is distressing?

The size of a table?

Why must spaces be kept clear?

Any precautions?

Any special treatment?

+

In general, never tell the tour guide
he is handsome.

How you will be paid
is for Sean Connery to answer.

Introductions are forthcoming
but to my discomfort.

Without reservation, the fancy jacket is above all
these evenings.

With so many children, where to stand
on candy!

Thankfully, your pleats
are settling better.

What can we say about the surroundings
they haven't said.

Either it's the heat or the line
is inching.

+

We are speaking on the condition
of anonymity.

Not our preference—this speaking
on anything.

Speaking on
something feels wrong.

Unless it's your brother.
Speaking on him is fine.

We could be talking podia
but that would be from.

Someday I might say I reflect you always
opening the door, which is sweet.

Short term I wouldn't mind being known
by you. If you'd have me.

+

Do not crumple it up. The night is young. You've got a star on your hands.

This is an important point. Hang on for a second.

I feel at time that way too. Does it rain just because what it does we say.

May I find another tissue.

There is no tea, I am afraid. How would you feel about another.

Trace over the field as quickly as May. That way I sense is best.

I learned when I stopped watching my feet. For sleep, thank goodness.

We have searched for ours. I hear those that reach all the way to the floor and up to the ceiling. Did you see the markings.

Our fathers and mothers were found of the lakes and trees and egrets. Where are they now.

That is quite precious, but I cannot stomach the lip. At your service.

+

Chemists have worked out
an optimum temperature
that takes into account all
factors involved, even comfort.
This is the temperature. It is
right in the center of the useful
working range and it is comfortable.
What is essential is an orderly
arrangement of the equipment.
Most comes in powder form.
The ability of time to control
density is based primarily on
the first few seconds which come
in powder form. This avoids
setting up a pattern of flow
across the face. The opposite
calls for emergency procedures.
The drawbacks are mathematical
sketches. Paper, like time,
curls toward the relatively
hinged side of the carrier
and his parcels. The coldest
tone is possible since all gray
is not simply gray. Inherently
cold subjects such as machines
ignite their surfaces like water
in general-purpose manufacture.
Simply turning an ordinary light
into winter places a boy on
a toboggan, into summer
and a bicycle. To be fully restored
requires the simplest application.
The cycle is a small car.

+

I do not need to babysit Friday and
I would love to go.

In light of our last conversation

I would like to go.
I like you.

I feel like we're in different places

+

How much per world. Is everything included.

The truth is we often settle for copies
and you got the one in the picture.

In the upper provinces
night will pull in soon and so begin undressing.

Just tell me you never posed for anyone or heard that question.

I cede reflections which are a stretch over time.
Did I forget myself and leave the sprinklers on.

The dolls and fields in which you leave them
are always underneath.

We have all lost a continent or two
and here bodies tend to pool.

+

Some are even petroleum-based. The rubber chicken's origins can be traced to the French Revolution, when soldiers were said to hang fowl from the ends of their muskets for good luck. Rubber drives during World War II are credited with launching the product line, setting rubber chickens in motion and into the hands of millions.

+

This is improving my death perception.

The shade falls on blankets
pulling west.

For the fixtures
we are thinking in that direction.

Feeling for contact is best practice.

The cities are frozen and packed
and you are stacking up.

We are always at the halfway
point to something.

Is this the house.
Are those daisies growing over the lip.

Now bear in mind
the child inside
drags behind.

This is also sound advice.
Try the grouper tonight.
I hear it divines.

+

Pineapples tell me
the season has come.

These days in all parts

the sky grasses
and tree hides.

There is a movement to drop it.

The ground we find
has a memory.

Night never arrives
or files the rocks.

The face goes for miles.

Each makeup running.

Many approach vanities
with water glasses.

I like others
noticed.

+

From deep in a hole of tequila
Fred announced

he'd like to mail himself to us
in an oversized box.

In the movie version,
Cary Grant, scanned in Trenton,

sliding off the package conveyor belt,
immaculate still after days of transport,

might have said: *Look away, darling.*
My bar code is showing.

No matter how they are stamped and handled,
these are fragile times.

Margins of error are one thing
and also another.

Which is to say
I may like everything about you

but you.
But I am still convinced.

That as it worsens,
the weather is getting better.

That there is news. And we are just the ones
to give it to.

+

A record for this time of year, set in 1969. Although an estimate, each figure is based on the data available. It may be a boy, a box, a flower, a rock.

+

And what has come over us.

The sky with clouds which science claims may require new names.

A case we have made for years.

What with developments in the fields and our shifting position on them.

Never a fluorescent X when you need it.

At the perimeter the wind lashing rockface until rain is phonetic.

From everything we are hearing, gathering ourselves and nesting.

The wasps outside the body and the wasps inside the body.

Humming over the dusk, a blanket tucked around us.

+

As for now, let's call it even.

A few beams and birds, respectively.

The cushions have been washed, delivered to the hotels.

There are mailboxes on the streets.

If you can, stay for tea, but explain that you must leave soon.

The teenagers did not study—

they are inside.

Someone from the living room may call out.

May hand someone a pastry.

Night falls in the palms, the stores open around the clock.

The rates of exchange,

the timing could be better.

To make the present and the present

continuous tense.

+

Not the first to arrive here by a long shot,
we conclude.

Waking this morning, traffic is in the air,
the forecast is for the birds.

A conflict has ended in papers,
the projections still ruffling some bangs.

The children come in to play dragging
their toys, the flowers collect themselves
and assemble.

And the pressure we feel here
and here, our body of patches and fractures,
this front settling around us.

From every direction the minutes drift,
each carrying a clear color photograph
of its form—

a line drawn at the end of the day,
the sheets on the line snapping dry.

+

According to a newspaper column, on March 19, 2011,
Canadian businessman Albert Chrétien, prompted by GPS,

was "probably trying to shave a few miles
off a road trip to a Las Vegas trade show

when he turned off Idaho 51 at Grasmere." "...[H]is wife, Rita,"
was "asleep beside him in their van." "[A]bsent from most maps...

the road dipped and twisted into a nightmare of steep-walled
sagebrush canyons and snow-covered mountains rearing

almost 11,000 feet into the sky." "The van lost traction and
skidded in the dark into a gully in the middle of a national forest."

"...the 59-year-old Penticton, B.C., resident walked into the wilderness
three days later, carrying a blanket...hoping to find help."

Nestled into the text is an image of the pretty, sunlit junction
at Grasmere, which the caption dubs "a ghost town." It calls

the mountains "lofty" and the road—or what for the Chrétiens
it would become—"slippery and treacherous." Telling this story is

reporter Richard Cockle, who also snapped the picture. "Travelers
should know that map data displayed by GPS units can be outdated,

with roads that no longer exist." Ultimately Rita lives, "rescued—starving,
dehydrated and cold—seven weeks later." Albert doesn't.

Acknowledgments

Much gratitude to the following publications, where many of these pieces (or earlier versions of them) first appeared: *American Letters & Commentary*; *Anti-*; *apocryphaltext*; *Bateau*; *Black Warrior Review* (online); *Copper Nickel*; *Dark Sky Magazine*; *Denver Quarterly*; *diode*; *Forklift, Ohio*; *The Laurel Review*; *Map Literary*; *The National Poetry Review*; *NOÖ Journal*; *The Oregonian*; *Portland Review*; *Spinning Jenny*; *Verse Daily*; *VOLT*; and *Washington Square*.

Thanks, great people at Spuyten Duyvil.

Susie! Stella! Love.

Notes

"+ [There is a glass of water]" includes borrowed/distorted text from Les Landin's *About Atoms: (Atoms for Junior)* (Scholastic Book Services, 1962).

"+ [Photography became a close collaborator.]" and "+ [Chemists have worked out]" include borrowed/distorted text from *The Print: Life Library of Photography* and *The Camera: Life Library of Photography* (Time-Life Books, 1970).

"+ [I never discuss love on an empty stomach.]" is comprised entirely of dialogue from Alfred Hitchcock's *North by Northwest* (1959).

"+ [What is the difference between an open coat and a closed coat?]" includes borrowed/distorted text from Roger W. Cliffe's *Woodworker's Handbook* (Sterling Publishing Co., 1990).

"+ [From deep in a hole of tequila]" is for Whiting.

The passages quoted in "+ [According to a newspaper column, on March 19, 2011,]" are from Richard Cockle's article "Those GPS 'short cuts' can be detour to disaster" (*The Oregonian,* May 15, 2011).

DAN KAPLAN is the author of *Instant Killer Wig* (Spuyten Duyvil, 2018), *Bill's Formal Complaint* (The National Poetry Review Press, 2008), and the bilingual chapbook *SKIN* (Red Hydra Press, 2005). His work has appeared in *American Letters & Commentary*, *VOLT*, *Denver Quarterly*, *Ninth Letter*, *Washington Square*, the anthology *Flash Fiction Forward* (W. W. Norton & Co.), and elsewhere. He is managing editor and poetry co-editor of *Burnside Review* and Burnside Review Press. He lives in Portland, Oregon.

CPSIA information can be obtained
at www.ICGtesting.com
Printed in the USA
FFOW03n1824080118
44350499-44060FF